Your Full Potential

Live the 7 Steps of How

Jo Le-Rose

Jo Le-Rose

Copyright © 2017 Jo Le-Rose

Discover Your Full Potential – Live the 7 Steps of How

All rights reserved. This book or any portion thereof
may not be reproduced or used in any manner whatsoever
without the express written permission of the publisher
except for the use of brief quotations in a book review.

First Printing, Createspace 2017

ISBN 978-1979809061

Cover Design: Sean Strong: seanstrong.com
Editing: Jools Bond - 007editing.com

Publisher: Jo Le-Rose
jolerose.com

DEDICATION

I dedicate the guidance in this book to the limitless self in each individual, that spark of eternal light and curiosity. I hope you find your way through the barriers of limitation to express all the goodness that you are.

CONTENTS

	Acknowledgements	i
	Welcome	1
	The Dawn of a New Day	5
	Preparation	7
1	What to Look For	19
2	Where to Look	47
3	How to Put it into Action	65
4	Troubleshooting	85
	Testimonials	93
	Further Reading	99

ACKNOWLEDGEMENTS

First and foremost, to the unknown: that deep, dark ocean of infinite treasure. My heart is out of the cage and my mind is open. There are no words to describe how I feel about you, my limitless self, the key of love to my prison door. Thank you.

To Mike: no other has given me the space that I needed to discover who I am. I deeply thank you for all that you do and for the wisdom and love that make up all that you are. I have yet to meet another who encompasses the great reservoir of light that you ceaselessly share with whomever you encounter. I love you x

To Louiza, Sam, Cheyanne, Ian, Isla, Nigel, Katie, Angus, Max, Mum and Dad: thanks for being you and for riding this rollercoaster of life with me and for the laughs, the endless chats, the many cups of tea and encouragement. I love you all x

To my dear friends: we've travelled a long and winding road together, filled with incredible experiences. This is what it's all about - the journey of lessons, laughter and love. Without you, I have no circumference, no mirror to see myself. You are me, as I am you. I hope the journey never ends and I get to love you all for eternity.

To those who were willing to trial the seven steps and ask the questions outlined at the end of each one: thank you for coming on this journey and for giving me the opportunity to observe the incredible effects these steps are having in your life.

Finally, to all those guiding lights who came before me, to those currently in my lifetime and to those who are yet to come: keep on making footsteps of freedom in the sands of time. I've learnt so much from you. My gratitude is eternal.

WELCOME

There is a plan and a purpose, a value to every life, no matter what its location, age, gender or disability.
—*Sharron Angle*

Thank you for choosing to read this book. I've always found that needed signs, messages and assistance show up at just the right moment. These are rarely by accident, but from an intelligent synchronicity, showing me that I'm on the right path. I would like to think that your attraction to this book is a sign that its content is meant for you.

I wrote this book, and others in the series, as a day-to-day guidebook for dealing with various life subjects. This specific book focuses on accessing your full potential and expressing it. For you to be reading these words, then there must be a sense that you're not yet living at full throttle. Perhaps you've felt that there's a more fulfilling way to live, but you can't quite grasp what it is or it feels elusive, non-reachable, or maybe the goal posts keep moving the second you begin to head in the direction of living your life purpose.

Those two words at the end of that last paragraph are easily bandied about, yet their meaning and power are often overlooked, so what exactly does living your life purpose mean? Perhaps we need to reword this and ask: 'What's the purpose of your life?' Surely, it's to bring forth your latent abilities and express them creatively in every moment, but few live at this level.

Why?

Because most people have suppressed their inner spontaneity under layers of social conditioning, so they accept the beliefs of others with very little questioning. What's a belief? It's a repetitive self-induced thought or a recurring instruction from those around you, which you believe to be true, even without proof. These thoughts become anchored in your mind when you attach a feeling of like or dislike to them. The stronger the feeling behind the thought, the more it manifests.

These beliefs began to be embedded in a layer of your subconscious when you were a child. Some of them were based on common-sense guidelines to keep you safe, but others had their roots in confusion and fear and these have caused the suppression of your inner fire of curiosity.

To live at the level of your full potential, the creativity in you will have to take risks and step into unknown possibilities. This is a natural movement as a child, but if you've suppressed it, at some point in your adult life there will be an inner restlessness, triggering you to ask yourself the following questions:

What's my life all about?
Why am I living the way that I am?
Why was I born in this country, in this family, race and culture?

If you don't delve into these questions and begin the inner search of who and what you are, then this restlessness can move into a sense of frustration. The older you get, the more you'll wonder if true happiness does in fact come from following what others expect of you and whether there's another way to live. Most mid-life crises are the eruption of this restlessness and frustration. Many throw out the baby with the bath water in their panic of knowing that they haven't fulfilled something and that life has been lived down a restricted route.

Traditionally, most of us are taught to:
Grow up
Obtain an education
Have at least a mediocre income
Buy a car
Find a life partner
Buy a house
Get married
Have children
Invest in life insurance
Die

I'm not saying that there's anything wrong with this general path, as there'll be many happy and rewarding events along the way, but you're reading this book, so you already feel that aspects of the above life are not for you. The restlessness is already there, a knowing that there's something more. It's time to answer this inner call by going within and investigating yourself. The aim is to find something unique or a passion for a subject that makes you want to get out of bed on a morning with a fire in your belly.

I've discovered for myself that there's more to life than just ensuring that I have a roof over my head, food in the cupboard and money in my pocket. These are basic and necessary things, but I know that the feelings you're looking for are freedom, happiness and a sense of being alive. None of these will come from dreading your day or being in a situation that drains the life force from your being. There's nothing more soul destroying than feeling that life is a monotonous drudge. This is where many slide into negative habits to find some form of relief, such as comfort eating, alcohol, drugs, gambling, etc., but this coping mechanism only brings more suffering.

It's time to discover just how incredible you are and exactly what treasures you have within you that have been silently working in the background. So, buckle up and let's go for a ride into the interior of you!

THE DAWN OF A NEW DAY

If you do not change direction, you may end up where you are heading.

—*Lao Tzu*

This book doesn't have to be long or bulked out with needless info. It just needs to get straight to the point by focusing on you and what you're perhaps not yet consciously aware of. These hidden facets of you have been guiding you and trying to nudge you in the right direction your whole life. Imagine if you'd known as a young adult **where** to look for what your full potential is, **what** to look for and then **how** to put it into action as your life purpose, all at an incredible pace. Do you think your life would be the same as it is today?

Your answer is proof that you have untapped potential.

The **what**, **where** and **how** are exactly what you're going to discover through the process of living through the seven steps detailed in this book. The question you may be asking is 'Do these steps work?' They've worked for me many times over and I've lived a colourful life. I've used these steps for everything that I've wanted to create, which has brought me global travel, vast experiences and the chance to meet incredible people.

Don't get me wrong, I wasn't born privileged. In fact, I grew up in poverty. I've been a single, hard-working mother, lived hand to mouth and really struggled to get a break. The seven steps were my ladder. Wherever you are in life, then I've possibly been there, so if I can steer my life down the route of self-fulfilment, then it's also something that you can do.

The seven steps are actually fairly simple. It's the execution of them that can be challenging. What's vital to their success is your ability to focus on the task at hand in every moment. If you can commit and follow through on all the steps, then you'll move towards the goal of living your full potential, which is the purpose of your life.

So without further ado, let's get you prepared for the journey.

PREPARATION

Intuition will tell the thinking mind where to look next.

—*Jonas Salk*

First Preparation – Know Yourself

Before we zoom off into taking the steps, there's something we need to be clear on and this is the two selves. The first self is the *limitless* you and the second self is the *limited* you. The limitless self is the you without any rules, limitations and boundaries. The place of ideas within you – your inspiration and the subconscious mind. The limited you is your conscious mind, which has been conditioned, so it's laced with self-preservation, limitation, right and wrong and what's expected. Both of these two selves need to be heard and acted upon. Each has a use and a rightful place. The limitless self needs to be able to flow unhindered and the limited self needs to assimilate information using its reasoning capabilities and act on any challenges.

However, if the balance of who gets to run your life leans towards the limited self, then you're character will tend to be over analytical, self-doubting and you'll often fear taking an action. The seven steps are therefore geared towards easing out this anxiety and prising open the mind to view other possibilities, bringing more of your limitless self into your daily life.

If you've ever blocked your inner talents and ideas from blossoming and allowed the striving for security to outweigh the impulse to take a risk, then your limited self has ignored the messages of your limitless self. Life is then lived down the route of habitual patterns, which prove to keep you hidden and safe. This is when the feeling of living a restricted or small life causes the restlessness to gather momentum. Therefore, the following warning is in all the books in this series:

Do **NOT** give your limited, conditioned self too much time to mull over the steps!

If you do, you'll find it goes a bit like this:

Limitless self: "Yes! I can get free! I'm going to be an interior designer!"
Limited self: "Well, that's three years for a degree, £20,000 in expenditure and possibly no work at the end, so why bother!"

The limitless self doesn't see anything as a limitation, only an opportunity to take an action that breaks through any barriers. The limited self prefers a life of non-disturbance, and as it governs the body, then it has the last say about any physical actions that need to be taken. If it worries, fears or hesitates, then you'll most likely give up on bringing forth your full potential.

Each step is designed to naturally lead you to further expansion, but you may be tempted to get into the flow and read the book through without doing the exercises. This runs the risk of just holding the information in an obscure storage part of your mind where it fades away and life continues in the same vein and you're still left with that sense of restlessness. To get the most out of the steps, stop at each one and complete it before you move on.

I can give you the roadmap to your full potential, but you must bring together your limitless and limited selves into the meeting ground of action.

Second Preparation – Use Fact as Your Friend

To assist the often turbulent encounter between your subconscious and conscious mind, the helping hand of fact is available. Used properly, fact can bring peace to the battle that often ensues between the impulse to act and self-doubt.

Fact can also miraculously transform situations, making the impossible, possible, but first, you have to discover what to look for. Fact itself isn't biased, so it doesn't take sides. It is what it is, so if you're in an argument with someone and you take away all the opinions of right and wrong, what will remain is the fact. This point of factual reference can bring clarity to any situation.

Using fact as your friend can greatly assist you to see what was previously hidden, but it takes courage to be willing to drop your end of the rope in the 'I'm-right-you're-wrong' tug of war. Try it. Take any situation that you're currently experiencing which needs resolving. Drop your angle on it. In other words, let go of your emotions and thoughts that hold you in an opinion and relook at the situation as if you're an observer of all sides. You'll find the fact underneath any personal preferences. This is the line of truth.

If you follow the line of truth, then the facts will resolve the issue - sometimes in your favour and sometimes not. This is when you may have to swallow your pride and mend your bridges, but fact is one of the best signposts that you can have.

The limited self is always looking for security and it fears the unknown. When a fact is seen, then the limited self can use it as a stepping stone to keep on moving forward, replacing fear as its new tool for life-guidance.

It's therefore vital to keep a check on your facts during the seven steps. Be honest with yourself. If you find that you're not sure how to answer a question or complete an exercise, look for the fact that lies underneath any indecisiveness.

Third Preparation – State Your Intention

Fact can keep you on the right path, but it's also important to be clear on what outcome you're looking for. There's a difference between wanting to fulfil your full potential and wanting to prove to the world that you're worthy.

The former is based on the joy of discovery and being open to making mistakes. The latter inflates the ego of your limited self.

1. Open – this is where you're open to new opportunities with a willingness to alter your direction at any time. The aim is to feel a sense of freedom in your ability to create.

2. Closed – this is where you're distrustful of others. Or there's a sense of urgency, in that you believe there's no space in the market for you and you fear someone will set out to steal, destroy or take from you, so you become isolated in your purpose.

The first thing you must do is set your intention to be open, as this is the signal to your limitless self that you're willing to listen and accept its intuitive input. The limitless self has a far greater overview than the limited self. It's the difference between the expansive view from the top of a mountain and the detailed view of a blade of grass in the valley. The limitless self can reach far and wide and draw in all that it needs from the collective subconscious. This connection is what brings you the needed people and events so that you can express your full potential. It has no fear, no judgement and it's unconditioned.

This is not to say that the limited self is without skills. It's the conscious accumulation of all the knowledge you've learnt to date and it has a real knack for dealing with details, but it's prone to worry about outcomes, so even that blade of grass can become a threat. Therefore, setting your intention to be open is to give yourself permission to grow in ways that you can't yet imagine. It's also the place where seemingly miraculous outcomes, meetings and events happen.

To make sure that your limitless self knows you're on board for the ride, repeat the following sentence out loud: ***'I want to live my full potential. I need to live my full potential'*** Repeat it over and over until your whole being is behind these words and you really mean them.

If you catch yourself being closed minded, secretive, rejecting help or pushing away synchronicities, you need to breathe deeply, let go of any worry about unknown outcomes or losing anything and restate your intention to work with your subconscious mind, your limitless self.

Fourth Preparation – Time is of the Essence

The present is shaped from the past, so if you don't think, feel, speak and act in different ways, then your future will look similar to today. If you look at your life and you don't like what you see, then it's crucial for you to master the one commodity that thoughts, feelings, words and actions all use - time. To do this, you're going to have to grasp what you've unconsciously been doing, so here's a note on where to begin seeing how you've utilised time.

It's Now or Never!

When you're mildly hungry, you potter off to the cupboard or to a café and you choose what you'd like from what's available on the shelf or on the menu. The hunger is such that you have time to ponder and choose, but when you get to that point of hunger where you'll eat anything, then all diets, fads and beliefs go out of the window. If you're in the Australian outback, you'll even eat grubs!

When something needs to be done, no choice is required, but when there's no urgency or time is involved, then choice can morph into doubt and indecisiveness, which can lead you into making a colossal mistake. This is where you need to learn to utilise time and not be used by time:

Dealing with time as 'now' = no choice = action
Dealing with time as 'future' = choice = delay

This is why you're not living your full potential right now, because your mind has been in a time warp of thinking that living your full potential will happen sometime in the future. The truth is, the expression of **your full potential is an action in the moment with your whole self behind it.** The whole self is when the limitless and the limited self are working together. If you find yourself dilly-dallying over choices, then the time of now, of urgent action, will slip through your fingertips.

This means that time and the flow of your full potential are powerfully linked, because the only true point of action you have is in this moment. The next moment is another point to create in, but if you dawdle in your choices, then you'll keep shifting your full potential to another point in the future, which you never reach, as all you have is now!

The conscious mind is always impressing the subconscious with what it wants, but you create your own reality by what you believe in. Belief is a repetitive thought backed by your powerhouse of feeling, so if you believe that freedom is in the future, when you get to any future point, freedom won't be there, as you still believe (think and feel) that it will be in the future.

This is how the future use of time has hindered you from bringing forth your full potential:

Young Adult:
Limitless self: I want to learn about astronomy
Limited self: That won't go down well with the family

Limitless self: I need to find a course
Limited self: Leave it until we have some spare time

Mid-Life Repeat:
Limitless self: I want to learn about astronomy
Limited self: That won't go down well with the family
Limitless self: I need to find a course
Limited self: Leave it until we have some spare time

End-Life Repeat:
Limitless self: I want to learn about astronomy
Limited self: It's too late

This repeat button is always putting your goals and markers at a future point when others will be happy about your choices or when the time will be right, but time is rarely ever perfect. Time is a window for action, so every second is a moment in which to act. Use it!

Dealing with time as now:

Limitless self: I want to learn about astronomy
Limited self: That won't go down well with the family
Limitless self: I need to find a course
Limited self: Leave it until we have some spare time
Limitless self: I will do it now

There's no repeat in the above, just action, which will lead to another action and so on. Within the windows of time, you'll complete the course and move on into vaster areas of learning.

The following three principles sum up your intention:

Be in this moment
Take an action
Focus on the goal

These principles are the very foundation of your journey through the seven steps. Not consistently applying these has brought you to where you are now, so the exit door to your current situation must be in applying them to your everyday life from this point on. Write these words on a piece of paper and stick them on the fridge as a reminder that you're committed to creating your life purpose of living your full potential.

This is your first test of not letting your limited self put off a task to some future date, so do it now. Even if you're reading this on the bus, in the pub or on a plane, rustle up a pen and write the words on the back of a ticket, a beer mat or on your hand. If you don't do this or you can't be bothered, then forget about reading any further. This book is not for you. If I told you that for five minutes only, the equivalent of ten million pounds in your currency will be deposited in your account, but you need to move it out within this timeframe, you'd make it happen! So, if you manage to scribble the principles down, then you've signed a contract for your part in the journey. Well done!

Fifth Preparation – The Microphone

On some of the steps you'll be asked to speak out loud and feel the emotional energy that comes from this action. This is an incredible tool and one that runs through the whole series of the books. Speaking out loud is not only cathartic, but it can give you a new perspective.

The way to effectively shift this energy and transform it is by fully sinking into the feeling and breathing through the emotional response. This allows the energy to move through you and disperse. The second you *think* about or *label* what you're feeling, you'll move away from feeling, so drop any thinking and go back to breathing through the energy. You'll need to find a safe, cosy place to do this.

Sixth Preparation – Your Journal

This is vital. Before you read the first step, type or write down exactly how your life is today on your current career/job level. At the end of the steps, you'll be able to compare any changes. Some of the steps require more time than others and some exercises are split into parts. Therefore, it's helpful to write your findings in a journal and keep track of your journey and schedule.

Preparation Summary – With your intention set, fact as your friend, the inner contract of the three principles, your microphone and your journal, you're ready for the off.

1

WHAT TO LOOK FOR

It is not easy to find something that will intrigue and bind your interest and enthusiasm. This you must seek for yourself.

—*Walter Annenberg*

The best place to start the venture of bringing forth what's inside of you is to ask yourself some vital questions. I recall the start of my journey from lack when I was living in poverty and struggling to survive. One day, after an experience of intense helplessness, I hit such a low that I basically screamed out in despair at the state of my inconsequential life.

This 'enough is enough' cry is a poignant moment. It represents a stage in your life where you can't take any more of the slog of trying to survive another day in whatever situation you find yourself to be in. The power of this 'get me out now or else' call is when your limited self has come to a point of such limitation that there's no wriggle room left.

The limitless self has been waiting in the wings for such an opportunity!

The second you reach that brick wall of frustration the only way of combatting it is by going through it. The release of that deep cry for help is what propels you forward and once the howl is over and you've shattered that brick wall, you'll find things will shift from that moment on. However, not everyone has to reach this point of acute limitation. Everyone has a different tolerance level. Some people only need a gentle prod to change direction and make another path their focus. However, the deeper your belief in being powerless, the more you'll reach an emotional crisis point.

Making another path your focus is the key and if you add in your friend of fact, you'll follow a very powerful singular line that leads you to a specific goal. If you get distracted, or ignore the facts, you'll scatter your energies. Therefore, to focus is to move in the direction of your passion and what you're aiming for comes into your now.

These next three steps are going to prime your focus and prepare you for moving your life towards its target.

STEP ONE – WHAT DO YOU WANT?

Everyone has a conflict inside of them, the conflict between what you should do and what you want to do.

—*Suraj Sharma*

What do you want? Four powerful words that only you can answer. When I ask people these four magic words, most reply with what they want for others or they describe wants that they have to fulfil to make others happy. For example, wanting a new truck for their partner's business or wanting to pursue a certain educational subject to keep their parents happy. These are not the wants that you need to focus on.

What do *you* want? Even if it means admitting that you want to do things others may be resistant to such as leaving a relationship or moving to a new house. This exercise is about you breaking through any type of censure from other people and giving yourself permission to be as limitless and as free as possible in the exploration of you.

Exercise Part One: Write down a list of your material wants. Brainstorm and challenge yourself to be as wild as you can in your choices. Once you've had fun in your freedom to want anything, you'll need to narrow the list down by eradicating any over-the-top desires. The list that is left will show the wants within your reach and the crux of your yearnings. Next to each item, write down why you can't have it. If you want it, then you haven't currently got it, so under the want is a belief in lack and this will be the 'I can't have it because...'

If you summarise your answers, you'll find three main reasons as to why what you want isn't present in your life:

Lack of self-power
Lack of means
Lack of time

The belief in being powerless to generate means to bring you what you want has caused you to use this moment as a point of struggle. This often brings with it a sense of 'Why bother. It won't happen.' The solution is related to utilising time effectively:

Committing yourself to the time of now = action
Action = better finances & health
Better finances & health = getting what you want
Getting what you want = your full potential

Using the microphone technique in your safe, cosy place, speak out on why you've avoided committing time to live your creative dreams or why the demands of others or general survival are taking up so much of your energy that you're left with a mediocre life. Behind the words, you may also have suppressed feelings of frustration, powerlessness, depression, etc. Whatever it is, sink into each one and feel it 100% until it moves through you and dissipates.

Exercise Part Two: Who is your #1 authority that keeps you limited? This is the person who conditioned you into believing that you can't have what you want and you also look to them for the recognition of your worth. You may immediately know who it is, perhaps a parent, peer or even a deity. Once you've located the source, go deeper to find out when their authority over you began. Speak out loud on what you think about this person and your relationship to them and feel any emotion that rises.

Whoever this #1 authority is, you've been allowing them to consciously or unconsciously direct your life. No matter what you do, you'll use this person as your gauge of worth and you'll always come up against them as an indicator of how well or bad you're doing. They're synonymous with any lack in your life, as you often fail to be recognised for your efforts and so you strive for more accolades to get their attention.

Behind the failure to get praise from this authority figure and attain the label of worthy lies another deeper core belief – a sense of feeling disappointed in yourself, which leads to self-dislike. This causes you to prove that you're good on some level, but this must mean that you're trying to springboard yourself out of its opposite of bad, which is a form of guilt.

This guilt is a deep sense that somehow or at some time, you did something wrong and now you're bad.

Observe your #1 authority and ask what you've been doing to appease them in order to receive recognition and praise. Feel how you've believed that they know what's best for you and then really look at their flaws as a person, their humanness and the fact that they too are looking to a #1 authority for their approval.

If you find that your #1 authority is a deity, then ask yourself how it's possible for a true deity to judge or have an opinion? If it does, then the deity is human-made and you're back to appeasing a belief. If the deity requires you to be a martyr and save humanity, then ask: Why does this deity lack the power to do it for itself?

Feel how you've possibly been held back in life by following the ideals of your #1 authority and visualise saying to this authority: 'I'm not here to please you or be deemed worthy by you. I'm here to express my creative talents and joy. If these don't please you, then that's your problem, not mine!'

Now watch what happens.

Summary: The first exercise showed that you can't have what you want because the feeling of being powerless is a stronger driving force than the feeling of want, so a battle between the two ensues and the stronger one wins. Lack is the result and it becomes difficult to bring what you want into physical reality.

The second exercise showed that underpinning your sense of powerlessness is the feeling of guilt for wanting something. You believe that it's bad to want and that you're not deserving of it, so lack is your punishment.

On a subconscious level, this thread of guilt runs through the whole psyche of human consciousness and it's related to a belief in some form of a deity. Even if you're not religious, subconsciously this guilt will be playing out in your life. It will take a huge realisation within the masses to lift off this belief in an authority who punishes and rewards behaviour. Karma, reincarnation, heaven, hell, ascension, spiritual hierarchy, etc., are all embedded in this human consciousness, which the limitless self absorbs the second it takes up a human body. This is reinforced by the race and culture it's born into.

Whether you're conscious of it or not, you'll have projected this inner deity from human consciousness onto an external source, such as mum, dad, boss, guru, etc. This person then becomes your #1 authority and you look to them to reward you with praise or to punish you with lack. If you were to visualise this inner deity and stand before it, you would feel exposed, possibly even angry or worthless, but under these reactions lies the feeling of guilt.

In truth, any deity that has an opinion or judges is human invented. It's not real. The limitless self would only have one question: 'Why are you limiting yourself?' It has no belief in you being bad, good or guilty, nor does it require you to save anyone or perform any task of service under the belief of being good. It requires you to get in touch with all the amazing qualities and gifts that are latent within you and bring them out into full expression. Therefore, the guilt is an illusion, a misplaced belief that you're here to please something or someone.

Challenge Yourself: *If you believe in lack, then lack becomes your reality.* This is a powerful sentence to ponder on. To believe means that you think it's true, even without proof. You deprive yourself because you believe that lack is an unchangeable characteristic in you, so you must live according to that truth. Behind it is a hypnotic instruction repeatedly given to your mind as a child until it became a habit.

Imagine watching a hypnotist show. Volunteers from the audience take their seats on stage and the hypnotist brings their minds into a relaxed state and then instructs them to act like bunny rabbits when they open their eyes. The second he clicks his fingers and they wake up, these 'normal' people start hopping around the stage and doing nose wiggles like bunnies!

Why?

A good stage hypnotist will raise your arm and see how you drop it to know how resistant your conscious mind is to relaxing and allowing in a suggestion from another conscious mind. Putting someone into a hypnotic state alters their brainwaves from beta through alpha and into theta. Here, suggestions are made to the non-resistant subconscious mind of your limitless self, and when awakened, the limited self obeys the command of belief sent from the hypnotic suggestion.

The conscious mind is the limited part of you that is externally focused and it communicates its needs to the limitless self who provides it with the exact match in the form of people and events. If you consistently send thoughts and feelings of lack and impress these upon your subconscious, then they will become your reality. The good news is that you can technically use your conscious mind to self-hypnotise yourself out of old, limiting beliefs.

However, the strength of feeling attached to a belief is the deciding factor. The limitless self is energy in motion. If it has been suppressed, then this powerhouse will be held in the body as a blockage, wrapping itself around the original thought that stopped its flow. No amount of self-hypnosis at a theta brainwave level will break it. To release the belief in lack, the repressed energy must be expressed through feeling it.

Challenge One: Speak out loud on how you feel about lack and how it affects your life. Pinpoint when you felt you were first hypnotised with it. Was it as a child listening to your parents' money worries? Was it in the realisation that your needs were not met? Or perhaps it came from wanting what others had? Whatever the initial hypnosis was, there'll be an emotion behind it. Allow the feelings to rise and breathe through them until they dissipate.

Challenge Two: When you feel that you've verbally and emotionally uncovered all the repression, then in your cosy place, sit or lie down and *very gently* tap the fingers of your left hand on a surface, so the arm of a chair, for example, or the mattress. Do this while relaxing every muscle of your body, apart from your fingers, as these will still be tapping. When your body is completely relaxed and your mind begins to drift, the tapping will cause your mind to stay slightly focused. This is the time to self-hypnotise. Begin to imagine your life with no lack and if you can, *feel* the freedom of having abundance.

When you've completed your visions and you're feeling full of abundant energy, then become fully awake by moving your body or you can do it just before sleep, making these abundant thoughts and feelings the last thing that you are aware of. Do this several times a week, but make sure that any repression in Challenge One has been dealt with first.

Case Study: Mandy was a bright young woman, but the shadow of hardship was already showing on her face. I asked her what she wanted out of life and she responded with 'I don't know, maybe a little house, so that I can escape my parents.' Mandy was living at her parents' home with her three-month-old son. I could see that she was despondent and had lost hope in her future.

For homework, I asked her to write down her list of wants. When she returned for the next session, she produced a long list of items and the shadow was gone. Excitedly, she told me that once she started thinking about her wants, she couldn't stop. Going through the list, we narrowed it down to what she really yearned for, but then the shadow returned and her eyes darkened. 'There's no use in trying,' she said, sadly. 'How can I get anything on this list when I don't even have an income?'

I asked Mandy who her #1 authority was. After some consideration, she felt her mother was the one who she looked to for acknowledgement. This also revealed the underlying belief that her mother had drilled into her as a child: 'Don't go living above your station.' Her mother had also become pregnant while young and struggled to financially survive. Mandy was going down the same route.

On speaking out loud about lack, Mandy felt that to reach for her dreams was impossible and that she was to shut up and put up with mediocre and be grateful for that. One of her major wants was to be a nurse. Taking just this one item from the list, we decided to use it as her main focus and build her whole life around it. Using the following six steps catapulted Mandy into realising that she did have the power to create a life beyond repeating her mother's pattern.

Questions & Answers

Q: I've spent my whole life caring for other people, so there's not much on my want list!

A: That's because you've never asked yourself the question before, so it may take a while for your suppressed wants to rise and be heard. Life needs to be a balance between caring for others and having care for yourself. Most associate self-care with physical elements, such as diet and hygiene, but there's also emotional and mental care. Asking yourself what you want starts the process of adding these two into your life.

Q: My #1 authority is god (who plays out in my dad), who is watching me and weighing up all I do. And so I self-sacrifice my needs to put others first, thinking that this makes me a good person and I'll be rewarded, but I still live in lack!

A: Any so-called god that requires you to be good, yet never rewards you, isn't really god at all, as you're still being punished through lack. By not receiving the praise, your belief tells you that you've not yet reached the state of being good enough to get the reward, so it becomes a vicious circle.

The point is, you're doing something to get something. It's the difference between doing something to appease an authority for worth and doing something just because you can. During the first one, you act whilst listening for that recognition. The second one is done just for the joy of discovery and sharing.

Q: Will self-hypnosis really work or is it just another gimmick?

A: Belief is a result of hypnosis, a repetitive thought or instruction, so looking across the globe, I guess hypnosis works really well! Try it, find out. If you complete the step and repeat Challenge Two often, and abundance does or doesn't show up, then I guess you'll know for yourself. The key is to have an open mind about it.

STEP TWO – THE TWO PATHS

If you don't like the road you're walking, start paving another one.

—*Dolly Parton*

The two selves of you, the limitless and the limited, walk two different paths. The limitless self walks the path where you'll find the true state of your being and the limited path is the avenue of your conditioning, which is mainly underpinned by a sense of seeking safety, living in lack, feeling powerless or believing you're guilty.

Exercise: Write down the journey of your two paths. To do this, think about how your life is today and what will happen if you keep on going down this same path that has been built upon your conditioning. This path limits your own ability to create abundantly. List everything, from your relationship, career, friends, family, etc. This is path one.

Now look at your list from step one of what you want. What will your life look like if these are a reality for you? This is path two. There will be a huge difference between the two paths. Now imagine each path is a sweater. Visualise wearing path one as a sweater and then path two. How do you feel? Speak the following out loud: ***'I choose path two!'*** Repeat it until all the power of your passion to be free is behind those words and you mean them. This is your intention to switch from path one to path two.

Summary: The rest of the steps will now be focused on bringing that path two into a reality. This is the potential that you came into this life to fulfil and it will occur from an inner shift. The outer always follows the inner.

Challenge Yourself: Imagine you and I are sitting in the best café in the universe having a cup of tea together before we embark on our journey to be born into this life. Whilst nibbling on cosmic cake, I ask you what you're going to do when you arrive on earth, what your life will look like, what talents are you taking with you to share, what do you want to accomplish, how you will make it happen and what effect you will have on the world. Really feel into these questions.

At the end of this life, we're going to meet up for cocktails and I'm going to ask you if you've lived the life that manifested the answers to the above questions or did your limited self get in the way? Did you get caught up in the human trap of conditioning and shut down your connection to your intuitive self and follow path one?

If so, you gave away your creative power.

It's important to feel for what you wanted to bring to this life and reset your course. Path one will keep you small, fearing your own power and worrying about the reactions from others. Path two is where your expansion is, your full potential. This is how your limitless self can affect your life. To accomplish it, you must have brought with you the tools – it just needs you to say 'Yes!'

Case Study: Mona was a hard-working accountant for a large firm. There was a serious air about her and life was organised down to the last full stop. I wasn't sure why she came into my space, as she seemed to have life all worked out. 'I don't know,' she said. 'It feels as though I've missed something?' I asked Mona what her favourite hobby was. 'I love trekking!' was her excited reply.

There was a light in her eyes when she said those words, so we expanded what that meant to her. Mona's inner dream was to be a tour guide for trekkers and hikers. Shocked at what came out, she put her hand over her mouth and laughed at the absurdity of it.

I asked her how she'd feel if she was living this alternate life. 'Free!' was her reply. I asked her how she felt in her current life. 'As solid as a rock.' The words surprised her. They fit perfectly with what her parents had expected her to turn out like, but there was still this inner restlessness.

These were her two paths and we deeply explored the contents, the feelings behind them and how she would look back on her life at the end of each path. Mona was amazed at the contrast. To her, path one felt dark, drab and safe and path two felt light and full of colour and unknown adventures. Realising that she had unexplored options, she felt that she couldn't go back to living the monochrome existence of path one. When I asked Mona what she felt she had come to the earth to do, she said, 'I came to experience nature, to be with it, explore it and share it with others.'

Mona decided to feel for the training needed to be a trekkers tour guide and once she had taken that first step onto her path two, she began to steam ahead. It took her two years to gather her full momentum. The last I heard, she was travelling abroad and living her path two.

Behind each path are repetitive feelings and thoughts. These attract to you the people and experiences required for you to fulfil each path. Therefore, it's crucial to master the direction of the mind and focus it along the lines of the thoughts and feelings that will benefit you.

Questions & Answers

Q: I've clearly seen both of my paths, but to get to path two I'd have to basically drop everything! How have I got so far away from path two?

A: Because you believe that path one is what you deserve. It comes down to your limited self, the conditioned part of you. It wants to stay small, safe and secure, so it believes that path one will bring that to you, but it doesn't. It makes you feel restless and often there's an inner ache, as if you haven't done something you were supposed to do.

It's never too late to move from path one to path two as technically, they are the difference between aligning your thoughts and feelings to either the conditioned you or the true you.

Q: How come my limitless self hasn't let me know and shifted me onto path two?

A: You're here, aren't you? The limitless self is energy in motion. If you've suppressed it, then it needs to be released to once again flow through you and outward as your point of attraction. It's a bit like locking up your twin in an underground vault, leaving him/her to traipse across the globe on aeroplanes and yachts and then wondering why your twin isn't with you.

Unless you use the same language as your limitless self, then you won't hear, see or know it exists. That language is feeling.

Q: *It's going to take me years to fulfil path two!*

A: Do you have anything better to do? You could spend your whole life wearing the sweater of path one, but you deserve a life full of all that goodness that's just waiting to be released and poured through you. The journey to fulfilment is where the joy is. The difference between the two paths is that on path two you're not alone.

Q: *Most of my friends have got big dreams, but not everyone's going to drop their bread & butter job to try and fulfil something on a seemingly fantastical scale?*

A: You've already rejected path two before you've even taken a step forward. Not everyone's path two will consist of building big empire's. Some people want to excel where they're currently at, so the next promotion or maybe a nurse wants to move into private care rather than public care or another may be looking for inspiration to greater works of art. The opportunities are endless.

What people want differs from person to person and if they follow the steps, they'll impress those wants upon the power of the limitless self, the subconscious mind and they'll make it happen. Don't be a spectator of life – *go and live it!*

 **STEP THREE – YOUR LIMITLESS SELF**

Your soul's desires compel you to grow, evolve and move closer to your highest potential.

—*Debbie Ford*

Knowing what you want, seeing the two paths of life lived from your conditioned state and what's possible from your limitless self, you'll be grasping that there are two clear ways for you to live.

Exercise: Write a letter to yourself from a future version of you who is no more than five years ahead. This future you has acquired everything from your want list in step one. Make the letter as detailed as you can and describe things such as your home, finances, family and partner. Spend a little more time writing how you're financing this new life and what your career looks like. Also, include how you feel about living this new life. Are you happy? Is life flowing? Do you feel there's room for more growth? If so, what growth would this be?

It's important for you not to read beyond this step until you've written the letter, as it will become the foundation of the subsequent steps.

Summary: This step pulls together the two previous ones and gives you an insight into a possible future version of you. Paths one and two are both vibrational in feeling. The two sweaters reflect this. These feelings are your powerhouse of attraction and they underpin your current material reality. If the feelings of guilt and powerlessness have been stronger than the joy to create, then your life will be showing manifested states of lack.

These three steps are taking you on a journey of ***what you want your state of being to feel like***. Re-read this, as it's so powerful. In truth, it's not really about the extra room for your home or the world trip, it's about your state of feeling, your powerhouse.

Challenge Yourself: Anything that you want has to make it through the filter of your belief in lack. To conclude this section of steps, take the life that you wrote about in the exercise and really go into what it ***feels*** like.

This state of feeling is your limitless self - this is what you're really after...

During the day, stop for a moment, remember the letter from your future self and immerse yourself in the feeling that it brings. Hold it for as long as you can, as this is your happy vibration, your highest state of being and the new vibrational platform from which you'll attract.

Case Study: Kasper was a young man with a lot of ideas for his future. Recently, he'd spent most of his money and time on following a popular manifesting course. Some of the things he'd focused on had materialised, but with the bigger, more life-changing items, he just couldn't seem to manifest them.

Kasper wanted a quick fix, so the thought of going through my complete program for creating a different lifestyle didn't fill him with great joy. All he wanted to focus on was how to get what he wanted. However, he quickly found that beneath his attempts at manifesting was a whole world of belief in lack and this was the block. Going through his beliefs and releasing the feelings of guilt, he came to the exercise of writing out his letter.

Once finished, he eagerly asked what would happen now. I asked him how he felt. 'Marvellous, excited!' he replied. I then asked him if he could recall a time when he'd ever felt so good. 'Nope!' he exclaimed. I then congratulated him and told him that all he had to do now was work on his feelings throughout the day until he was living in this state of being most of the time.

The light seeped out of his eyes and his shoulders hunched. 'Is that all there is to it?' he mumbled. Now I was excited. I asked him if he could say in one or two words how he'd mostly felt during the day in the past. 'I felt as though I were plodding along,' he replied. I then pointed out that his life was fulfilling his feelings, so he'd been plodding along! The light was back. Kasper had his 'Aha!' moment.

Questions & Answers

Q: What I've written in the letter to myself is exactly what I've wanted all my life, but I've never got there, so what makes you think that I can do it now?

A: Because lack is not your natural state of being. What you're discovering is just how much you believe lack to be true. Physical reality is a result of what you believe in, so the external moves to create that belief. The truth is, you felt your limitless self, so you're already there. The physical difference between where you are and where you want to be is that you don't live at feeling this frequency for more than 80% of your day, so it doesn't materialise.

Q: Trying to remember to be in this feeling throughout the day is just too hard and I keep forgetting!

A: It's because you've lived in the habit of being unconscious of your feelings and thoughts for so long. At first, knowing what's happening for you mentally and emotionally in every moment may feel like a mighty effort, but as you consciously catch yourself in your old program of conditioning and shift yourself into the new zone of feeling your limitless self, it will get easier.

Q: By constantly shifting myself into this point of attraction, will I manifest the life in the letter that I've written to myself?

A: In proportion to the percentage of your day spent living in it and utilising the remaining steps, then you'll manifest your state of being. If a higher percentage of your day is spent in an unconscious stream of thinking and feeling lack, then you'll manifest that state of being.

UPON REFLECTION

The first three steps will have taken you through the mire of your emotional world, from seeing:

1. What you want and why you can't have it
2. The two paths
3. What you're really looking for

If you've flicked over these steps, then try not to read any further until you can go back and cover them and every nook and cranny has been explored.

Putting the Picture Together: We began Chapter 1 with what to look for. Finding your wants and focusing your thoughts and feelings throughout the day at the vibration of your true self is the completion of your search. If your inner world creates your external life, which the case study snippets also show, then your new state of being will be affecting your material world. What you've realised is that the world really does reflect you and your hidden beliefs, which have been subconsciously attracting in the very people and experiences that perfectly reflect what you believe you deserve. The good news is that by living at the level of your highest state of feeling, which is your limitless self, then life takes on a whole new perspective, as your point of attraction will have shifted out of lack and onto fulfilling your path two.

Test It: When you're feeling this high state, notice the changes that occur in your environment or in the people around you and how you're much more likely to smile and share joy than when you hold yourself in the vibration of path one.

The Results: The more you educate yourself into living within this higher vibration, which holds everything from your list of wants, the more synchronicities begin to occur in your life. Doors that were closed before begin to open or you meet the right people as if by chance. The limitless aspect in you is living and connecting to others from its expanded view, so your physical life is assisted to meet with the new vibration.

Now you've discovered what you're looking for, the next step is to discover where the point of creation is in you.

2

WHERE TO LOOK

He who does not know how to look back at where he came from will never get to his destination.

—*Jose Rizal*

It's such a relief to know that you're at the forefront of manoeuvring your own life down the route of feeling for your limitless self and that you don't have to follow what your ancestry dictates to you. Most get this far, in that they discover how their thoughts and feelings affect their physical world, but few know how to consciously work with them. A bit like seeing that a fork-lift truck can carry the heavy load you want moving, but not knowing how to operate it.

Physical manifestation and outer experiences help you to see how you're doing, but inner reflection is the only true place to look for your own power, tools and creative inspiration.

Your life isn't some random happening nor is it meant to be inconsequential. Before you took up human form, your limitless self made a blueprint of what it wanted to achieve. This included a specific quality that you were to bring into everyday life and use to shape your journey. Along with your true state of feeling, this quality is what will bring you the greatest joy.

Therefore, the next set of steps begins the process of utilising the focus on your highest feeling into altering the outer effects. This will prove to you just how you've been subconsciously creating all your life and it will give you the confidence to know that you do have an input as to your daily outcomes.

STEP FOUR – GLIMPSE THE FUTURE

I want people to be blown away when I do what they don't expect.

—*Drew Barrymore*

Most of what you've been discovering has come forward from a layer within your own subconscious. The future will unfold according to your beliefs and you're adding to this outcome by what you like and dislike or what you repel and attract. Follow the exercise to see just how this 'repel and attract' from your past is currently building your future.

Exercise: Look at the first home that you moved into when you left your parents' or carer's house. Make a list under the headings:

What you felt
What you had
What you didn't want
What you did want

If you've only ever lived in one place, then use the above headings as a time scale, so if you're 25 years old or under, the headings would list the first three years in the property and every consecutive three years after that. If you're 45 years old and under, the list will cover five years and above 45, it will need to be seven years. If you've lived in many houses, then choose at least three that had the most emotional impact on you. Start with the earliest one until you reach the place you're currently living in.

The examples below are taken from my experiences. To show you the flow, I've made mine very simple, but you can add detailed information. It's fun to see how these details change!

First home (or first block of 3, 5 or 7 years):
I Felt:
Unsafe/frightened
Alienated from my neighbours
Stressed

I Had:
My own car
Lovely things
A full-time job in healthcare
Close friends/social life
Physical health

I Did Not Want:
To live in this dark area
To be amongst drug dealers, thieves and bullies
To financially struggle on my own
To be alone with the huge responsibility of parenting and working full-time

I Wanted:
A supportive partner

Better finances
To live in a better area
To feel safe
To learn something new

Moving on to your next home **(or second block of 3, 5 or 7 years)** follow the same process.

I Felt:
Safer
Stressed from the extra travel to work with a small child
Happier having neighbours

I Had:
Lovely things
A new career
A supportive partner
Better finances due to supportive partner
Close friends/social life

I Did Not Want:
Imposing neighbours
Another child, which my supportive partner wanted
To live in this small house
To live in this semi-dark area

I Wanted:
Extra income
An extra room for my business
To live more in nature

Again, you can continue and you'll see a pattern emerging:

Third home (or third block of 3, 5 or 7 years)
I Felt:
Very safe
I was healing my past
Happy living in the country
Happier with less imposing neighbours

I Had:
A new car
An office for my business
A promotions company
Etc.

If I reach where I am today, I can look at my list and see EXACTLY what future I'm building!

Summary: This exercise clearly begins to show how what you don't want and feel strongly about starts to be replaced in the new or current home with what you do want. This means that your ability to emotionally and mentally attract and repel are very powerful.

Challenge Yourself: When you reach where you are today, look at what you're saying to yourself about what you do and don't want. This will be your future, so make sure you add your new wants from step one to your list.

Case Study: Jean came into my space with a feeling of life being humdrum. Now in her mid-fifties, she was questioning whether she'd really done anything useful with her time. Jean left her parent's home at sixteen to get married and then spent the next thirty-six years living in the same house. At first, she couldn't see how the exercise would help her, as she didn't plan on leaving her home or making any huge changes. On writing it down in blocks of seven years, it astounded her to see how she'd been creating her life along the lines of what she'd consistently repelled and attracted.

The results revealed that behind her seemingly normal life of being married to the same man, having two children and living in the same premises and even the same street all of her life, she was an actual creator. In one block of seven years, she wrote that she didn't want to live in a small space anymore and in the next block, they'd built an extension. There were many other happenings that occurred from her lists of wants and don't wants. This excited her, as she realised that she could expand herself into smaller details and bring them forward as strong desires, attracting or repelling them. Needless to say, Jean got busy and life didn't feel so humdrum anymore.

Questions & Answers

Q: My ability to create was so clear to see! Why didn't I know? What exactly was I doing to make it come about?

A: You were doing what comes naturally, moving towards something or moving away. This is done subconsciously, but belief is what stalls you and causes you to hold on to what you don't want or what doesn't work. The aim from this point on is to consciously create by using your natural abilities to manifest your true state of being, which is your point of attraction.

Q: I'm confused! I've just gone bankrupt and lost everything and now I'm staying at a friend's house. I've gone from everything to nothing, so how did I make that my future?

A: Go through the exercise again, very slowly and when you get to your last home, really look at what you were saying that you didn't want. Perhaps it was the responsibility, stress, any debts or you felt out of control. To crash at this level says that you were spreading yourself too thin in trying to hold it all together. What you wrote under 'I did not want' will reveal why you're in this position. Under the listing of 'I wanted' is what you'll be moving into.

Q: What about other people in the home, do they affect what happens as they too must be doing the same thing?

A: Yes, although children have a lesser input as to the decisions, they make it known when you're moving away from what they want into more of what they don't want. As parents, we often overlook this and hope that they'll settle down. It's vital at this point to communicate.

Most people attract each other due to the frequency that they live at, so they generally hold the same beliefs and want similar things. This makes it easy to move from one home to another. If one partner changes their frequency or one is stubborn about listening to the needs of the others, then they'll create an imbalanced home. In many relationships, there can be a dominant partner who insists on wanting things their way, so the other partner often feels uneasy when expressing their wants. In the end, they'll do one of three things: resist and cause explosive arguments, put up and shut up, which stifles their own creative essence, or leave.

STEP FIVE – YOUR QUALITIES

Quality is not an act, it is a habit.

—*Aristotle*

Some people can walk into a room and just uplift it with their presence. Other people can take a problem that appears to be insurmountable and solve it without effort. Then there are those people who make you feel safe. They have a quiet strength about them. None of these people are special, they're just naturally expressing who they are and they couldn't hide their abilities under a bushel if they tried. Their limitless selves are shining through their personalities. Now it's time for your limitless self to shine.

Exercise: Write a list of all your characteristic qualities that are emotionally based. For example: playing music is a physical ability, a passion for music is a characteristic quality. Read through the list and you'll find that there's no belief of lack behind these qualities. This is who you are and your highest expression to others. If you feel your way through this list, it will bring you a sense of what's available to you from within. For example, here's my list of qualities:

I love to freely spend time with people
I love to share
I leave others feeling uplifted

I'm passionate about bringing out the best in people
I love to solve problems

From the given example, I can clearly see that the common denominator in all of my characteristic qualities is helping people reach a better potential of themselves.

Look carefully at your list. Can you see what common denominator is running through your qualities? Write it down.

Summary: This common denominator is the very thing that you want to express fully in your life. In truth, if you were to let this out without any resistance, then your reality would shift all by itself.

The more you express this common denominator, the more the doors of opportunity will open for you. However, it's best to find the right route of expression for you or you'll end up wasting time with unnecessary actions.

Challenge Yourself: In step three, you wrote a letter from your future self describing the life you'd be living if you were to follow path two. This brought forth from you a feeling, which is the true state of your being – the energy and vibration of your limitless self. The common denominator is the true quality of your limitless self. This is what it came into physical life to express.

If I asked you to feel your true state of being and your common denominator, they'd be the same feeling, as they're one. The second you take the action of your common denominator, your limitless self is being expressed.

Throughout the day, feel for your true state of being and perform the action of your common denominator. It may just be a smile at a stranger or the telling of a joke. Whatever it is, be conscious of doing it and how it makes you feel.

Case Study: Sanjay was such a gentle young man. There was an aura of nurturance about him, but his belief in being a failure was blocking his ability to share his common denominator. We spent some time going through the first four steps, but this step is where he became emotional. His qualities were that he loved to care for children, so taking his young siblings to the park, making up games and helping them with school work all came naturally to him. However, his #1 authority, his father, deemed him not manly enough.

When Sanjay realised his common denominator was one of support, he felt such relief, as this was his true self trying to get out. The only time he felt real happiness was when he was expressing this care. By working through the remaining steps, Sanjay built up a powerful platform of inner trust and confidence in himself and took a big leap from working in IT to training as a school teacher for young children. Sanjay left my space with big plans to make learning fun!

Q: My common denominator seems to be bringing joy to people, but I also suffer from heavy bouts of depression. Why such drastic opposites?

A: Welcome to clearly seeing the two paths. Depression usually occurs when you're not fulfilling your true state of being or not expressing your common denominator to others. However, this would seem contradictory to those comedians who suffer these very same highs and severe lows. The second the last bow has been taken and the stage lights are switched off, they nosedive from a high of joy into a deep depression. This is because the energy from the audience has become a drug, as what they, and you, are really running from is a deep-rooted loneliness.

This is not a human loneliness from a lack of company, but an inner alone, whereby no-one can reach you, as if you're in a cocoon of isolation. The book on relationships in my series would assist you in dealing with this.

Q: How do you hold the feeling of these qualities or your limitless self throughout the day?

A: Do you remember writing those three principles to use for the steps?

Be in this moment
Take an action
Focus on the goal

You follow these principles by becoming conscious of your thoughts and emotions in each moment and making the necessary shift to alter your frequency.

Q: My common denominator is kindness. I've always loved animals, as they're so easy to relate to. I work with them as a vet, but I'm shy with people, so how do I reach out?

A: This may sound strange, but can you see people as you would an animal? Have you ever read the Tao of Pooh by Benjamin Hoff? The characters take on the personas that are similar to humans, so why separate them? Don't you deal with emotionally hurt animals, fearful ones, excited ones, nervous, aggressive, lost ones, etc.? How do you treat them? I'll bet with kindness.

Most humans you meet are covering up what animals show so readily and openly. If you can see them beyond their human façade, you'll deal with them on the level that is your natural quality.

UPON REFLECTION

The previous two steps will have shown you where to locate your potential for creating, which comes from knowing what you do and don't want and from discovering your inner qualities:

1: Proof that you've been creating subconsciously
2: Your qualities have a common denominator

If you've flicked over these steps, then try not to read any further until you can go back and cover them so that every nook and cranny has been explored.

Putting the Picture Together: You know what you want and you know how to challenge your #1 authority and the beliefs that tell you that you can't have it. You've found the energy of your limitless self, clearly seen the two paths and now you've proved to yourself that you can create what you want and remove what you don't want. The key from this moment on is to do it all consciously.

Test It: Walk through your home and look at all the things that you don't want or what you want changed. What is the feeling behind each item? This feeling is a vibration and it's this that you really don't want in your life. Hold or touch the object and allow any resistance towards it to move through you as a feeling. Breathe deeply through the process. Once you feel that it has shifted, look at the item again and see if there's still a resistance. This action alone will begin shifting what you don't want from your life at a detailed level.

The Results: You truly are the director of your own experiences. Everything comes down to energy and vibration, which you know as your thoughts and feelings. These two avenues can be consciously used to move energy in and out of your life. The fastest and most powerful way is to focus and be in your true state of being and apply your common denominator at every opportunity.

3

HOW TO PUT IT INTO ACTION

A dream becomes a goal when action is taken toward its achievement.

—Bo Bennett

The previous chapters have been easy to navigate in the process of uncovering the hidden facets of you. Now it's time to take the mental and emotional work from the steps and channel them into physical reality. The final two steps are designed to get you moving in the right direction and make your letter in step three a living reality.

The *how* to do something always requires a starting point, a learning curve, a journey and the meeting of the goal. It's easy to give up at any of these junctures, but if you're determined to live your full potential, then the *how* to do it is the point where you can excel.

The limited self, or the conditioned part of you that believes you're not worthy or that you're powerless to bring about change, is going to give you a few headaches during the shift from path one to path two. Thoughts may pop up on how useless you are and how you won't succeed. This is where you need to cling on to the *how* in these next two steps and just keep on moving forward.

When you chose to come into this world, you wanted to express yourself in a limitless way, to bring forth your qualities and capabilities. There was never any doubt about you being able to do it. What's got in your way is the belief that others know better for you or that you need to live a life based on security rather than creative endeavour.

The **how** is your way out.

 **STEP SIX – THE ROAD TO WALK**

Create a compelling vision, one that takes people to a new place, and then translate that vision into a reality.
—*Warren Bennis*

The exercise below can really define what's going on in your subconscious and how this relates to your qualities and path two. It uncovers what the best avenues are for you to express your common denominator.

In the previous step, you dealt with your characteristic qualities. Now it's time to look at your other skills, so write two lists, with the headings *Physical Abilities* and *Mental Abilities*. The abilities below are taken from my own lists:

Physical Abilities – I Am
Strong
Flexible
A dancer
A fast mover
A landscape painter
Artistic
A writer
Good with musical instruments
Good at singing

Mental Abilities – I Am
Quick thinking/intelligent
Excellent at memorising
An avid atomic science fan
A problem-solver
A deep thinker/philosopher
Good at developing the inner self
Interested in health/medicine
Interested in property design
Imaginative
Good at reading music and symbols

Once you have your lists, you'll be able to see various possible avenues, some unexplored, others lightly dipped into, and these will be your core interests. By taking one or two physical abilities and joining them with their mental counterpart of a similar interest, you'll see how I could have had several possibilities of expression:

The Road to Walk – I could be:
A physical worker in a fast-paced industry
A dancer
A musician/singer
A property/interior designer
An atomic physicist
A self-development teacher
A healthcare practitioner
An artist
A fiction/philosophical writer

My life has gone down many of these avenues in an unconscious way. I've worked on an assembly line, in health care, in management, as a counsellor, as a painting instructor, etc. In fact, I could turn to any one of them and give it my full focus and bring it into fruition.

Summary: This exercise brings forward the subconscious possibilities that your limitless self has open to it in this lifetime. Creating your new reality is now getting exciting because you can choose any one of these and have the full backing of your powerhouse!

Challenge Yourself: To see the favourite road that your limitless self prefers to walk, go back to step three. Once again, look at the letter that you wrote to yourself. In there, your common denominator will be tied to the dream career that you wrote about. Look at your list above, as the same possibility will be there. This is your road to walk.

Mine was writing and teaching the subject of self-development to uplift people into their limitless self.

Case Study: Claus worked as a teller in his local bank. Soon, he was to be made redundant, as the bank was closing its branches to expand its online services. Claus didn't know what he was going to do, but he felt that if there was ever going to be an opportunity to make a career change, then this was the time to do it. Still living at home with his supportive parents, Claus had no other family responsibilities, so he had a little personal and financial breathing space.

Breezing through the first two steps, Claus suddenly stalled on step three. It took him a while to really write about his career in the letter. I had to keep reminding him not to block it with what other people wanted for him, but to focus on what he would want if there were no rules. A lightbulb seemed to go on in his head and he completed the step.

Claus found that his common denominator was mainly focused on the emotions behind his hobbies, so he loved to make old things work again, like watches and clocks. In this step, he found that his physical and mental abilities were based on his keen eye for detail, steady hands and he loved reinventing things that people had cast out. Other work possibilities had been a cyclist, a librarian and an antiques dealer. All of them had the task of looking after equipment or old items.

When he checked back to his letter in step three, he was living by the sea above his own workshop that had a vintage storefront. Inside, he was reinventing and selling old bicycles with modern twists, bringing the old and new together. This was the preference of his limitless self. If he were to go down this route, he was being shown that his business would be successful and he'd be living a fulfilling lifestyle.

Questions & Answers

Q: I'm actually doing something mundane, which is also on my road-to-walk list. I'm shocked though, as another one on the list is my passion, yet it feels like one of those out-of-reach dreams. Now I'm wondering whether to pursue it.

A: If it's on your list, then it's a possibility for you! Why don't you take the first step of researching all about it and what you'll need to do to make it a reality?

Q: I can see that I've flitted in and out of all my roads to walk and not really focused fully on any particular one, so now I feel like I've wasted precious time.

A: I wonder what caused you to stop what you were doing and then shift to something else? Was it the fear of success, the fear of failure, not wanting responsibility? What was it? This is the emotional block that needs to be explored and brought out.

Q: I can see the dream that I always thought was out there is actually right in the room with me! There's nowhere to hide from it now, but I'm

worried that I'll do what I always do, set off with zeal and then fizzle out. How do I keep up the enthusiasm?

A: When a person discovers a new idea or enters into a new relationship, they experience an initial surge of excitement, but when daily care is required to keep those fires stoked, the excitement dwindles.

It takes daily work and commitment to your path two to make what you want happen. This will not include striving or competing against others. It is done by knowing that you have the talents within you and the support of your limitless self, which includes working with your subconscious. Turning within and working directly with your path two will bring you synchronicities, as the limitless self has a wide influence across the whole of mind. It will assist you when you centre yourself in this moment and keep your focus on the needed action and the goal.

Q: For the first time, I feel there's hope. I've been dithering about what to do and how to do it and now I've got some clarity, but how do I bring it from an idea into real life?

A: You tackle the bear in step seven!

 STEP SEVEN – TACKLE THE BEAR

Everything you want is out there waiting for you to ask. Everything you want also wants you. But you have to take action to get it.

—*Jules Renard*

Armed with your true state of being, your common denominator and the road to walk, it's time to take the action to get yourself from path one, across the ravine and onto path two. To do this, you're going to need to build a map of your step-by-step process.

Most people panic when they get to this part. All the previous steps have been mainly emotive and mental. This step requires physical action. I call this action 'tackle the bear.' What does this mean? Perhaps this morning you woke up and went into your kitchen to put the kettle on, only to find a big bear taking up most of the space. What did you do? Maybe you froze in terror? Or screamed, turned and ran! The bear, nonplussed by your reaction, decided that it would like to stay.

To get the bear out, you're going to have to lure it out. If it comes out all at once, it may pounce on you and basically, you'll be toast! The key is to tackle it slowly, piece-by-piece, so, from around the door comes first a paw. Once you're familiar with it and you know how to handle those claws, then in comes another paw. By tackling it one piece at a time, it becomes less overwhelming and threatening.

Your letter from step three is the bear. Reading it, knowing that your aim is to reach that place, can feel like a tremendous task to undertake. By breaking it down into manageable pieces, you'll feel more inclined to do the work to reach your destination.

Exercise: In your safe, cosy place, breathe deeply until you feel calm and at peace. Now reread your letter and ensure that your road to walk corresponds with how you're financing this new life. Then write a list of all the actions needed to make step six a reality. This may include things like training, equipment, financial help, etc. Brainstorm and write down every detail that you can.

Now put the details in a chronological order. This needs to be done by using backwards time. To do this, look at your letter and work backwards on the process that it took to get you there. Make the timeline no longer than three years.

To give you an itemised course of action, split your chronological order down into at least five threads. For example, maybe you want to write a bestselling self-help book with a website platform to hold your blogs, podcasts, products, etc. To do this, you'll need to split your chronological list into five threads - finance, IT, products, courses and marketing.

Using the example of the threads – break it down into days:

Day One
Step 1 of IT – Get a URL name
Step 1 of finance – Price up website hosting
Step 1 of products – Write draft of book
Step 1 of marketing – Research the book market
Step 1 of courses – Draft online courses

Day Two
Step 2 of IT – Website hosting/design
Step 2 of finance – Cost of editing/book cover
Step 2 of products – Continue with book draft
Step 2 of marketing – Build a two-month launch plan
Step 2 of courses – Do a trial video or recording

These blocks of five steps are what you're going to take every day. Some steps will take longer than others, but you just continue with them until they're complete. You can take more, but five is the minimum.

Summary: Just from the example above, you can see how each day you'll progress towards what you wrote in your letter in step three. If the ravine between where you are now and where your limitless self prefers to be is huge, don't panic! I've been in this situation and I was riding on the bear's back, hanging on for dear life. I gave up my full-time job, which was my financial stability, and enrolled at university.

I didn't know how it would turn out, but I needed to take an action. It was a drastic one to take and I could have gone part-time first and then tackled a paw of the bear, but I didn't have the knowledge of this step back then!

Some of the actions are going to fill you with trepidation, as you're going to meet with many self-doubts and steep learning curves. The strength comes from the realisation that you only have this moment to make a difference, which builds your next moment. So even if you want to put your head in a hole and forget about any steps, know that you're on top of a breakthrough and this is the most crucial time to act.

It's also imperative to do these steps as an addition to your current lifestyle, so don't sneak in steps that need to be on a to-do list for your day, such as go to the hairdressers, pick up the dry-cleaning, etc. Separate your threads away from your general to-do list.

I also used a business model as the example, but you may have included a new relationship in your letter, so you can use the same backwards stepping of time to see how and where you met and what extra self-care steps got you there, such as joining an online dating forum or taking a confidence-building course. Make it fun to add this in as a thread.

Challenge Yourself: Make at least one of those daily steps a leap, so a bigger part of the bear or a more difficult part, such as the jaw! Another helpful task is to write or speak out a conversation between you and your limitless self that covers the steps to take. In your safe, cosy place, imagine another version of you is in the room with you. This version is the wise part of you, like your very best friend. The conversation needs to start off with what you're frustrated about and it must be candid because your limitless self is not emotionally invested in your life. Here's how my chat panned out:

Me: I need to get out more and help people!
LS: Do something about it then.
ME: Like what?
LS: Advertise your skills somewhere, so people can come and see you.
ME: Yeah, but I don't fancy having a physical office anymore.
LS: What about an online service?
ME: That would work, but how would I deliver the content?
LS: Take a group on a journey and help them to sort out their problems.
ME: What? Like coaching or creating a new reality? That sort of thing?
LS: Yes, as you have some serious skills.
ME: Like what?
LS: You have all the emotional, mental and physical tools plus vast info on how consciousness works.

ME: Okay, so I build a program for them to follow.
LS: Yes, and make it so that they can get results quickly.
ME: Ah, like steps. Do I just get straight into it or do I need intro sections on how they got into situations in the first place?
LS: Apply the tools that you used to get out as steps, then explain how they got trapped in later sections.
ME: So, the other way around to the norm!
LS: Yes, action first, explanation after.
ME: This is even better! Thanks.
LS: Then you can turn it into a book.
ME: What? As in how to change your reality in a number of steps?
LS: Yes, short intro, the steps, case studies, quotes, Q&As.
ME: So, would I include all the levels of the emotional, mental, physical and consciousness or would I separate them?
LS: Do steps for every subject of life.
ME: Wow! I wouldn't have thought of that! Will it work for the readers?
LS: It worked for you, didn't it?

I wrote this conversation after my life crashed and I had to sell the health retreat that my partner and I had owned in France. I then spent four years facilitating online courses through live webinars and workbooks, the content of which is now part of my series of books for living. In your conversation, you'll also receive insights as to the best action to take. This tool can also be used on any subject, so relationships, disputes, illness, etc.

Case Study: Kate had worked out exactly what she wanted to create, but every time she set out to take an action, she'd freeze in fear. All her self-doubts would come piling forward, not to mention the negative remarks from her family on how pointless her dream was. It went against the grain of the generations of solicitors and accountants as Kate wanted to be a health coach.

The problem was, Kate was unhealthy herself. She was 22kg overweight and didn't know the first thing about health, but she had a passion for food! Kate had done all the steps up to this one. The thought of tackling even the bear's paw was as terrifying as being locked in a cage with one. Kate would break out into a panic at the thought of giving up her safe career, diving into unknown territory and being her own guinea pig.

Kate's conversation with her limitless self was incredibly revealing. At the beginning, she told me how she'd spent a good hour crying through her frustration, but by the end of the conversation, she found herself feeling really excited about what her limitless self had to say. Five threads emerged and her limitless self gave her the avenues of what she needed for her education:

Learn about health
Learn about detox
Learn about diet
Learn about exercise
Learn about support

From this, a whole program developed and she began taking five steps every day, one for each category. Kate found it be an absolute revelation! At first, her steps required her to read, join online courses and learn as much info as she could find on the subjects. This whet her appetite and she began to take control of her life by acting upon her new learning, which changed her habits, body and emotions. At this point in her journey, she was still working as an accountant, but each day brought her closer to living her path two.

The aim was to work part-time in accounting and set up evening classes in her hometown for women out there who felt as she had done.

What an inspiration!

Questions & Answers

Q: Okay, so it took me ages to break it down into five steps a day and now I have them, but some of them require me to have funds that I don't yet have. How do I get around this?

A: Have a conversation with your limitless self and see what is uncovered. The key is to not fret about money that you'll need on day twenty, but to look at what you need today, as this is the step that you're on. Also, you can't take a step whilst living in fear or with a feeling of lack either. The limitless self is a bit like an older, wiser version of you that has all the keys to your treasure trove. If you're open and you're working your way to expressing the true state of your being, then help will arrive!

Q: I found it easy to use backwards time, but my steps are like massive leaps?

A: You've not broken it down properly. Some will require a leap, such as signing up for that course or whilst working full-time, committing your evenings and weekends to the other steps, etc. If the steps are too big, see how you can break them down.

Q: I've done every step up to here, but I just can't do this one. Why?

A: Everyone gets stuck on a step somewhere, simply because that step is where the challenge is. It's possible that you're a 'tomorrow' person, whereby everything that needs doing is put off. If this is the case, then start practising the art of taking action by writing out a daily to-do list that covers the basics of your life. Make sure that everything you put off for 'tomorrow' is where you challenge yourself and consciously take the action immediately.

After seven days of doing this, you'll start to feel confident and more self-empowered about taking action, so then revisit your daily five steps that make step six a reality for you and it won't look so daunting.

 **UPON REFLECTION**

The final two steps will have taken you through the process of realising that path two is focused on the capabilities of your limitless self. You have everything you need from within you to make living your full potential a reality:

1. The avenues open to you
2. The steps that will take you there

If you've flicked over these steps, then try not to read any further until you can go back and cover them and every nook and cranny has been explored.

Putting the Picture Together: If you're living your life written in step three, then you're obviously expressing and creating from your qualities and available abilities. It's living from this point that brings you the opportunities for wealth and happiness. No-one else is responsible for bringing these to you. *There is no-one more powerful in your life than yourself.*

Test It: The only way to test just how fast and far you can move in a single day is by taking just five steps on your list. Once you realise that you can do it, an inner passion is ignited because you see that true power comes from acting in the moment. You can alter your life just by a single action.

The Results: When you put all seven steps together, you can see how you can keep on building, expanding and maintaining anything you set your mind to. Your reality is built on what you believe and this is based on what you accept as true. The second your life starts to move in the direction of your path two, any limiting beliefs will be challenged, because you'll realise that living a stunted life is a lie, as you've always been a Creator.

4

TROUBLESHOOTING

> I want to be intentional about my freedom - in choosing it, honouring it, and protecting it. One of the best feelings I know is feeling truly free.
> — *Kristin Armstrong*

At the beginning of the book, we set out to discover that the purpose of your life is to live your full potential and this book provides you with the *how*. These seven steps are designed to take you on a journey to reveal what you want your life to be like and to prove to you that you've always been subconsciously creating. This means that if you consciously utilise your common denominator down an available route, then you cannot fail to reach your goal in the letter from your future self.

The contents also clearly point to two paths and you have a choice of which one to walk. Path two requires you to take a gamble and break free of limited thinking, so by taking just five steps a day, you'll move forward at an incredible rate. However, some steps won't always be easy and things can go wrong.

The second you find something isn't flowing, you need to go through the following troubleshooting points.

If Something isn't Working
There are two reasons you won't reach what's written in your letter from step three:

1. Not enough action is being taken.
2. An ineffective action is being taken.

#1 comes from fear and self-doubt.
#2 comes from being inflexible.

These two problems are going to crop up a few times and this is when it's tempting to throw in the towel and decide that you've failed.

There is no failure – only an action that either isn't working or not being taken properly.

When you reach this plateau of being stuck, here are a few suggestions:

Combatting #1
1. Re-read your letter from step three to give you the realisation that this life is waiting for you.
2. Go back through step seven and make sure that you're not taking steps that are too big. If they're leaps, then break them down further into more manageable actions.

3. Prioritise – if you're not taking the steps because other avenues are demanding your attention, then split your day into sections. For example: one section for socialising, home, self-care, bills, etc., one for work and one for building your path two. When it comes to the time for your threads, make sure everyone knows that you're not to be disturbed. This doesn't have to be in one block. The best time to feel inspired is usually early in the morning, so perhaps rise earlier than usual to complete tasks that require quietude and then give yourself a little time when you arrive home for those tasks that require you to connect with people.

4. If you're not taking steps because you hit an area of challenge, then the only way out of this is to bite the bullet and take the action. A challenge is an area where you feel that you have inadequate knowledge or you're falling short of what's required. What you need at this point is research/education or to reach out and ask someone for help.

Combatting #2

1. If you're repeating an action and it's not providing you with any results or with negative results, then you need to stop taking that action.

2. For one day, let go of any steps and have some fun. Take a walk in nature, go for a meal or go to the cinema. Do something that takes you away from the problem.

3. When you've been away from the problem, look at it with fresh eyes or ask someone trustworthy to look at it for you and get a different perspective.
4. Do the opposite of the action that isn't working. This will release the resistance and generate a new outlook. For example, if you're designing a book cover on a free platform, such as Gimp, and you can't quite get across the seriousness of your topic, draw a funny cartoon! The opposite action is to bend your mind out of its rigidity.

The final problem that you may encounter is the vague syndrome. This is where the description of how you're financing your new life from the letter in step three is vague. If your new life is based on projects of philanthropy or voluntary work, then you need to look behind these to see where the finances are coming from to support them. If it remains vague, then your road to walk in step six will throw up avenues of confusion. This will cost you valuable time, so go back to step three and dig deep until you find how you're financing your new life.

The quicker you deal with these three points that can lead you to give up or lose valuable time, the quicker your project will move on. Every challenge you meet means that you're on top of a breakthrough, so you must keep going, as what's on the other side of it is generally a greater leap to reaching the fulfilment of your path two.

The Top of One Mountain is the Bottom of Another

As you near your goals, you'll see that you can go further and into more expansion. The growth is limitless and this is the time to redo step three.

In writing a new letter to yourself from step three, you may find a whole different scene emerging and you realise that your first letter was a platform to an even greater possibility. You can use the same process and build your steps upon the new vista.

It's also okay to reach your goal and stay where you meet with your initial letter, but it's important to use the same process of the five steps a day to maintain your current level. The second you stop taking those steps, problems will creep up on you, such as overdue payment days, out-dated IT, loss of website visits and so on. Therefore, it's vital that you maintain what you have built.

Remember the Three Principles
Be in this moment
Take an action
Focus on the goal

If you consistently apply these three principles to the five daily steps, then you'll understand their place in the journey of this book. In truth, there is only this moment that's available to you and it's imperative that you use it to bring more of the limitless you into expression.

If you scatter your energies, think too far ahead, worry about outcomes or put off today's actions, you'll stall and fall back into your old patterns, which is going back to wearing the sweater of path one. You owe it to yourself to keep going and bring forth a life where that inner restlessness no longer wakes you up in the middle of the night.

Only you can do it!

My Last Words
I use these steps every day for the projects that I'm building. They work and they can seriously bring what you want into your life. The only person that can stop this from happening is you. You didn't pick up this book to forget about its contents, you picked it up to bring the steps into your daily life.

Most of what you've read is a fairly simple, yet powerful process. If used correctly, the steps can bring you an inner discovery of alignment with your limitless self. Everything is a vibration. Wearing the sweaters of path one and path two clearly reveals this. What you're doing is shifting yourself into **_BEING_** the vibration of path two, where your full potential has an avenue to be expressed and materialise what you want.

Although the steps are straightforward, to act upon them will be the most challenging, but if you focus on the line of fact, take the action and deal with anything that's not working, you'll shift any blocks and move forward.

I've had an amazing journey applying them to all my creations and I would love to hear how you progress. Please look at the other books in the series and join me on my Facebook page and post your findings: https://www.facebook.com/selflimitless/

I wish you every success on your journey to expressing your full potential.

TESTIMONIALS

'Dear Jo, The changes these steps and your guidance have made for me, my life and my business are out of this world. The steps are so easy to implement in my daily life - and they are day-by-day, taking me one step further up the ladder and closer to my goal. At the same time I feel focused, clear and powerful. I have never been as much in the moment and so true to the inner me and I am in awe. 'Thank you' will never be enough.'

A Gammelgaard - Denmark

'Dear Jo, I'm deeply grateful for these amazing 7 steps. The precious wisdom you've shared and the step-by-step program have really helped me understand myself more and have shown me how to create a life of joy and freedom. I'm really looking forward to carrying on using the toolkit to go deeper and to live that joy in every moment. Feel it's going to be an exciting year. Thank you.'

J Bond - UK

'Jo, I have never felt so clear and focussed in life. The simple exercises show you how to look deeply at issues in life that are holding you back in a gentle but effective way that I have not found anywhere else. And then by applying the daily five steps, I now have a detailed map of how to live my ideal life. These 7 steps are absolute gems that have transformed my life. My deepest thanks!'

C Mathers - Australia

'Jo, you have guided me through every step of the way - literally step-by-step - and it has been clear, simple, mind-blowing and profound beyond words. These are steps for life - ongoing in every way, every day. I've realised it's not an armchair process for the 'can't be bothered'. It requires my input, honesty and willingness to take even just small steps, yet the effect on so many areas of my life, and the lives of those around me, is leaving me gobsmacked. It's like taking my light out from under a bushel, blowing away the cobwebs and then using that light for what it was truly intended for all along in life. Thank you for sharing your years of research, experience and numerous talents and gifts with such humour, kindness, immense clarity and grace. It really does mean the world.'

T Hawkins - UK

'Dear Jo, These steps that you have shared have been incredible. They've broken down mental and emotional blocks and I'm paving my way into an amazing creative future. I'm now on the path that I have always dreamed of and I don't think I would have ever got there without your inspirational teachings. I will be forever grateful.'

J Wynn - UK

'Dear Jo, The steps you gave were easy to follow and the effects are huge. I have the feeling that these are never-ending. They continue and if I need to, I can always go back to the first step. I am well on my way to the next business platform. One of the effects that amazes me the most is this deep, inner knowing that everything is all right. That all I need to do is to follow the next step and the next. I have absolutely no doubt, no worries, no speculations. Instead, there is an awareness, an openness to listen to the next guidance. It has made my life so much easier – and more interesting. I can't thank you enough.'

G Donnerborg - Denmark

'Thank you for these incredible life-changing tools that you have given us. At last I feel I am free of the shackles that were holding me back and I have a deep inner knowing about what I want to do and where I want to go with my life. Using the steps, I am at long last creating the life I have always wanted, the dream that was always there inside me, and I am eternally grateful. Thank you.'

J McDonnell - UK

'Dear Jo, When the opportunity arose to suddenly try out the steps in this book, I knew then it would be special. At every turn, you were there. It was like someone was reading my mind and knew exactly what it was that I needed to realise in each moment; where I was stuck. The tools are life-changing and I certainly know my direction and that there is plenty more to come. I look at life with different eyes these days. A heartfelt thank you.'

S Flowers - Isle of Wight

'Dearest Jo, I just wanted to share with you how the steps have changed my life right from the first 10 minutes of starting them. There's a constant inspiration in me now which, no matter what is happening in my life, is always there behind the scenes, urging me on. I use the steps and tools in everyday life; it's my personal tool bag, like a best friend. Each step and action I take is opening doorways and paths to such amazing and joyful experiences, big and small, which I could never have imagined. It is so much more than seven steps, it's a lifestyle.'

A Tyrer - UK

'Dear Jo, I am filled with gratitude that I was able to do these steps and for your guidance at the beginning of what I know will be an amazing journey. I found it easy to understand and have no doubt it will change my life. It has uplifted me and inspired me to take steps I wouldn't have done before. You are a very gifted and generous teacher, down to earth and with a wonderful sense of fun. Thank you with all my heart.'

C Stell - UK

'Dear Jo, I found the 7 steps to be the impetus I needed to get out there amongst all the locked-away dreams held inside. The tools learned were very easy to follow and gave me the ability to tune deeply into feelings. Taking the steps, going back over my journal notes, and challenging myself with things that have an unknown outcome made my knees knock together sometimes, but it has led to change. These changes include moving away from areas that weren't necessary and expanding more fully into areas that are. These seven steps feel like a parting of the waves to the things I love and feel the most limitless with.'

K Wise - Australia

'Having done the 7 steps, I just looked back to the notes in my journal. I was not in a good space! 2 months later, the lightness, the clarity I feel is incredible. It feels like so many weights have been lifted from me and I can see the way forward. My house is up for sale, my business is up for sale and I have let go of so many things that were suffocating me. This may sound extreme to some, but I have taken the steps needed that have been clearly shown by my limitless self to realign me to my path two, which is freedom, doing what I want to do business wise whilst offering my family a wonderful opportunity to share in this too. Without these steps, I would have certainly suffocated by now. It was no way to live a life. Now, life is finally exciting and flowing. Thank you, Jo.'

K Wells – UK

FURTHER READING

Life-Guidance Books by Jo Le-Rose in the 7 Steps of HOW Series:

Series 1: all to be released by early-2018
1. Discover Your Full Potential – Live the 7 Steps of How
2. Manifest Your Goodness – Live the 7 Steps of How
3. Cultivate Inner & Outer Success – Live the 7 Steps of How

Series 2: all to be released by mid-2018
1. Heal Thyself – Live the 7 Steps of How
2. Resolve Your Relationships – Live the 7 Steps of How
3. Build a Balanced Body – Live the 7 Steps of How

Series 3: all to be released by late-2018
1. Dynamic Parenting – Live the 7 Steps of How
2. Developing Your Consciousness – Book 1
3. Developing Your Consciousness – Book 2

Printed in Great Britain
by Amazon